W9-AFT-339

BE GREEN!

AN ACTIVITY BOOK FOR YOUNG PEOPLE
WHO WANT TO SUSTAIN AND PROTECT
THE WORLD WE LIVE IN

STUDIO
PRESS

STUDIO PRESS

© 2019 Studio Press

Written by Mandy Archer
Illustrated by Katie Abey
Designed by Rob Ward
Edited by Frankie Jones

978-1-78741-462-4
Printed in China   0240119
1 3 5 7 9 10 8 6 4 2

An imprint of Kings Road Publishing
Part of Bonnier Books UK
The Plaza, 535 King's Road, London, SW10 0SZ
www.studiopressbooks.co.uk
www.bonnierbooks.co.uk

MIX
Paper from
responsible sources
FSC® C010256
FSC
www.fsc.org

THIS BOOK BELONGS TO

_ _ _ _ _ _ _ _ _ _

WELCOME TO BE GREEN!

We all live under the same shining sun. We are all global citizens of the same world. This activity book has been designed to help you to think of ways that we can look after it together.

The world is an enormous place and it is easy to feel very small, but every person counts, every single day. Drawing, colouring and writing in this book will help you to think about how you can connect with others to protect our precious planet. You can start anywhere in this book – pick any page that catches your eye and start scribbling. How and when you spend time with this book is completely up to you. This is your space to dream, think and doodle creatively. Sometimes our best ideas come when we find a quiet time to relax and let our mind wander. Curl up with this book and have fun!

We should all care about the environment. As the population gets bigger, the world faces more and more pressures. Pollution in our oceans, climate change and threats to wildlife are all big problems that are going to take time and patience to solve. Sometimes thinking about the future of the planet can make us feel worried and helpless. When an eco-problem seems big it can be hard to see a way forwards. If you feel like this, remember that you are not alone. Young people all over the world are already reaching out to each other to make real, effective changes to help to save the environment. Talk to a grown-up you trust at home or go to see your teacher. They will help support you and look at positive ways we can work together as global citizens.

There are also lots of amazing organisations and initiatives that will help you on your journey to being green. Many are setting up schemes in schools and local communities, too. Perhaps they will inspire you to take action or start an eco-scheme near you. Spend some time with a trusted adult and go online to explore the websites below:

THE WORLD WILDLIFE FUND

The WWF is the world's leading independent conservation organisation. Their mission is to create a world where people and wildlife can thrive together.

www.wwf.org.uk

ECO-SCHOOLS

The largest environmental schools programme in the world, Eco-Schools engages millions of children across 64 different countries. Ask your teacher if you can get involved!

www.eco-schools.org.uk

EARTH DAY NETWORK

Earth Day is aiming to build the biggest environmental movement on the planet. More than a billion people take part in its activities each year.

www.earthday.org

THE WOODLAND TRUST

Protects and campaigns for the UK's woodland, planting new trees and restoring ancient woodland.

www.woodlandtrust.org.uk

OUR FRIEND, THE EARTH

The Earth gives us a home to live in, food to eat, medicine to heal us, water to drink, air to breathe, and energy to run our machines, towns and cities. It is more important than ever to treasure and protect it.

WHAT IS THE ENVIRONMENT?

When we talk about the environment, we mean everything in the world around us. This includes the air, water, plants, animals and food chains.

ONE AND ONLY

The Earth is the only planet in the Solar System with exactly the right conditions for us to survive. It is not too hot, nor too cold, allowing it to support life.

NATURAL HABITATS

The Earth is very diverse. There are mountains and deserts, forests and oceans, ice caps and grasslands. This rich variety provides homes for countless species of plants and animals.

Colour in our amazing planet

UNDER THREAT

Over the course of many centuries, the Earth's human population has grown. We have had a massive impact on the environment in which we live. We have created pollution on the land, in the skies and in the seas.

CLIMATE CHANGE

One of the biggest consequences of pollution is climate change – the Earth is warming up faster than ever before. Scientists believe that this warming could seriously disrupt the way that our environment works.

ALL CONNECTED

The Earth is finely balanced. The water cycle, weather, plants and animals, and the passing of the seasons, all work in harmony with each other. A small change to any of these can affect others massively.

WE'VE ONLY GOT ONE EARTH. IT'S OUR JOB TO TRY TO PRESERVE THIS UNIQUE ENVIRONMENT. LET'S DO IT TOGETHER!

THREE IS THE MAGIC NUMBER

Being green doesn't have to be hard – in fact, it's as easy as one, two, three with this fun bingo game!

Just remember to
REDUCE, REUSE and RECYCLE:

HOW TO PLAY:

- Look carefully at the bingo boxes. Each one contains a mini challenge.

- Colour in a square every time you achieve the goal inside.

- Can you complete a line of squares in under one week?

1 REDUCE

Buy less and buy smart. Cut down on the amount of rubbish you personally create.

2 REUSE

Instead of throwing something away, give it to someone else or reuse it all over again.

3 RECYCLE

If an item really does need to become waste, dispose of it properly!
Try to recycle everything you can.

Help to put the recycling bins out.	Buy something you need from a charity shop.	Put all of your food waste in a separate bin to the main household rubbish.
Save your leftovers to eat for lunch the next day.	Turn the tap off when you brush your teeth.	Customise a piece of clothing that you don't wear any more.
Walk somewhere instead of taking a car.	Swap magazines with a friend.	Refuse a plastic straw in a café or restaurant.
Put on a jumper instead of using a heater.	Wash old cans and bottles before you throw them into the recycling bin.	Go through your old toys and give them to someone else to play with.
Mend something instead of replacing it.	Use a refillable water bottle.	Take a shower instead of a bath.
Persuade your family to buy food with less packaging.	Turn your computer or TV off at the wall instead of leaving it on standby.	Donate your old books to the school library.

COLOUR IN THIS SLOGAN USING YOUR BRIGHTEST COLOURS:

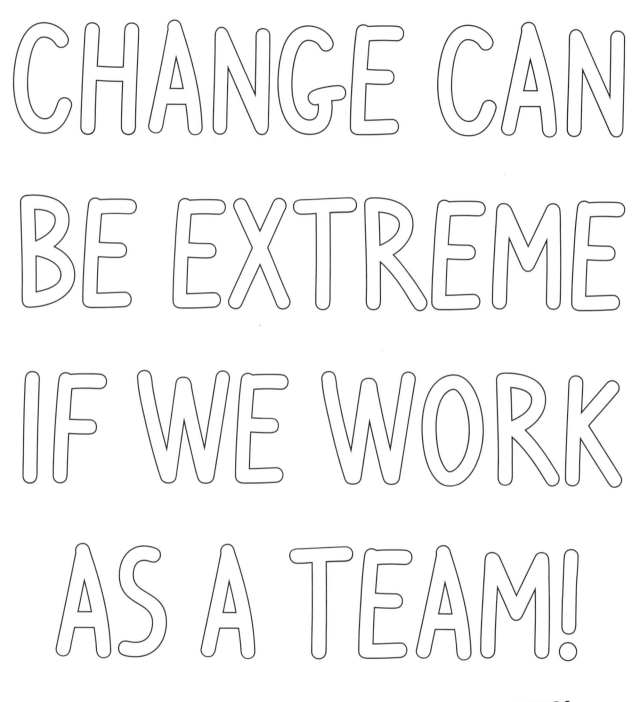

CHANGE CAN BE EXTREME IF WE WORK AS A TEAM!

WHY NOT GET SOME FRIENDS
TO HELP YOU?

BIRD'S-EYE VIEW

Climate change doesn't just mean that the world is getting warmer – rising temperatures can also cause surprising and extreme weather events. This is bad news for birds. In these conditions, they have to fly away to somewhere safer.

These birds are on the move. Can you draw the weather being described in each view?

FLASH FLOODS

FOREST FIRE

HEATWAVE

HURRICANE

HEAVY SNOW

ELECTRICAL STORM

What other extreme weather have you spotted in the news or on TV?

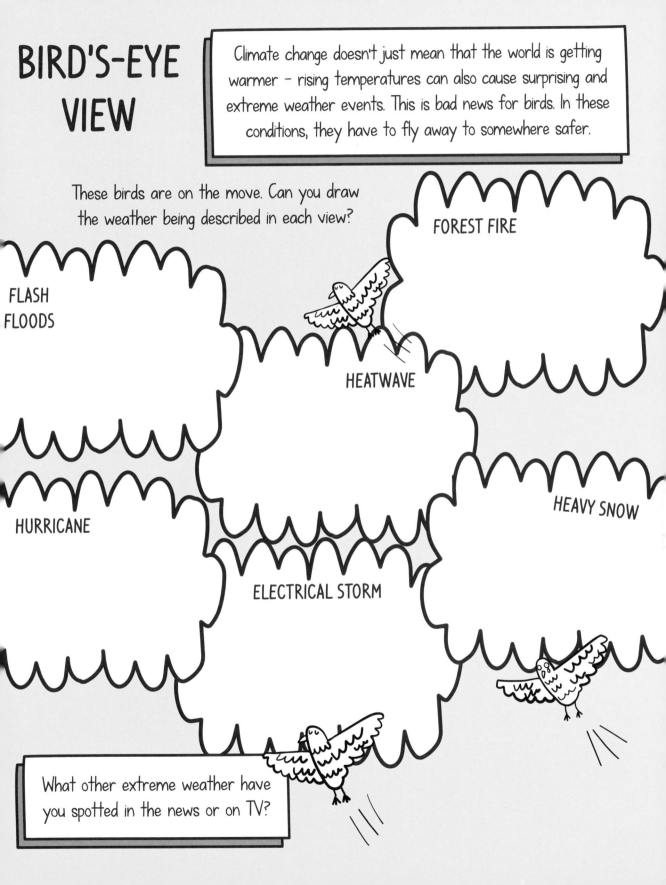

IT'S THE LITTLE THINGS

One small act can inspire many more!
Do something green today and the effects
of that action could travel far and wide.

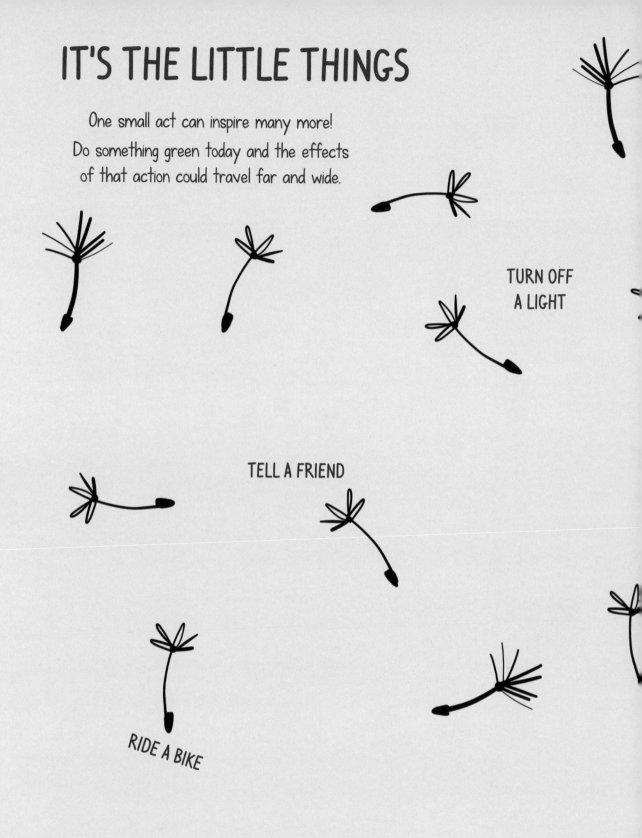

TURN OFF
A LIGHT

TELL A FRIEND

RIDE A BIKE

The seeds from this dandelion clock are being blown by the wind.
Who knows where they will reach?
Write a little thing that you could do today for your planet beside each seed.

PLANT A SEED

DOORSTEP NATURE

Nature is everywhere – even if you live in the tallest tower block in the biggest city! Use this page to draw pictures or stick in photos that show that you have all kinds of wildlife living near you.

Leaf

Shell

Grey feather – it could be from a pigeon

Blue-and-white butterfly

Animal tracks

Ask an adult's permission before you go out nature hunting. The green rule is look but don't touch!

When you get home, however, it's always a good idea to wash your hands.

BRIGHTEN MY WORLD

Use your sketching skills to transform this unloved patch of land into a sensational space.

BEFORE

Plant trees, take away litter and introduce some wildlife!

AFTER

POTTY ABOUT FLOWERS

Plants are important for humans and all living things. They release oxygen into the air, create food and help to clean our water system.

When flowers bloom, they also fill our day with colour!

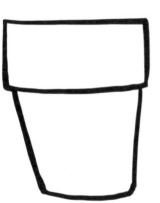

Grab your brightest pens, then draw some brilliant blossoms in each pot.

MAKE AN INSECT HOTEL

Insects are tiny but vitally important for the survival of all animals. Be kind to the bugs near you by making an insect hotel for them to shelter inside.

WHAT YOU NEED:

- A large plastic drinks bottle
- Any of the items below that you can find in your garden or the local countryside:

Twigs	Bamboo cane
Tree bark	Nuts
Acorns	Pine cones

WHAT TO DO:

1. Ask an adult to cut the plastic bottle into at least three sections. Each section will form a room in your bug hotel.

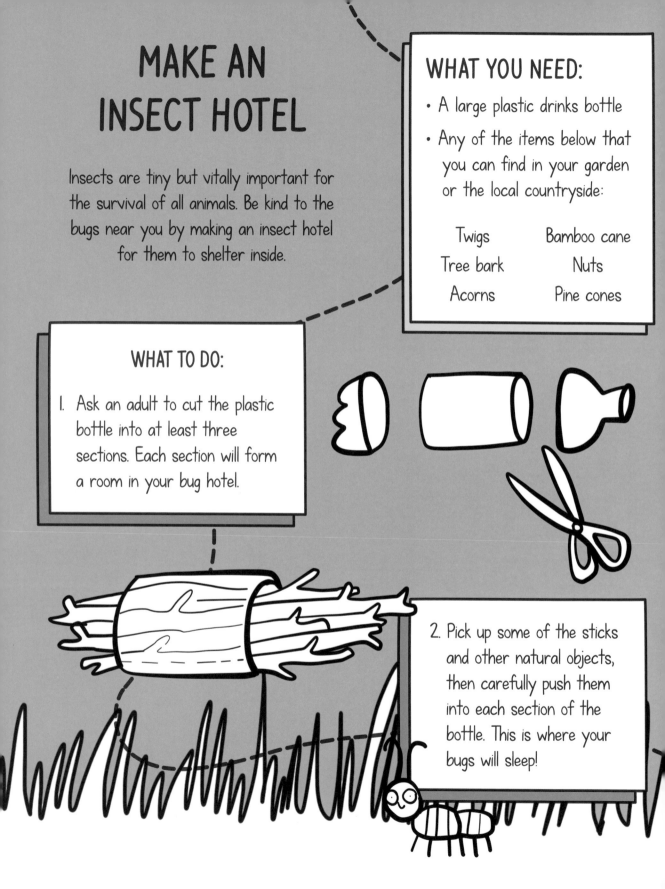

2. Pick up some of the sticks and other natural objects, then carefully push them into each section of the bottle. This is where your bugs will sleep!

3. Keep slotting in little pieces of bark, twigs, nuts and pine cones until each section is full. Don't try to cram too much into the bottle – the bugs will need some room to creep and crawl around.

4. Find a quiet, shady corner of the garden or an outside space, then line up the sections of the bottle. Your bug hotel is ready for visitors!

Be sure to get permission before you set your hotel up, especially if you want to place it in a public area.

WHY DO INSECTS MATTER?

Bugs and creepy-crawlies are the largest group of animals on Earth. They pollinate plants, provide food and help to break down waste.

ONE STEP AT A TIME

Do you get a lift to school? Are there other ways you could travel there, reducing the pollution the journey makes?

What about walking, scootering or riding a bike?

If you live too far away to cycle or scoot, have a careful think. Could you share a lift with a local friend or ask your parents about taking the bus?

Draw a new way of travelling that you would like to try:

What route would you take? Make a map to your school here:

Plot your route with a dotted line.

ECO-VEHICLE

A fossil fuel is made by burning the remains of plants and animals that lived long ago. Coal, oil and gas are all examples, but the Earth's resources won't go on forever. This type of fuel also creates enormous pollution.

How will we get around without fossil fuels? It's up to you to design the blueprint for a new, greener car, ship or aircraft!

POWER UP! Where will your eco-vehicle get its energy from? Brainstorm some ideas here:

UNPACKAGING

Look inside the supermarket trolley.
Write down some ideas for how each item
could be packaged without lots of unnecessary
plastic, cardboard and cellophane...

WRITE YOUR OWN
PLASTIC-FREE SHOPPING LIST

PLASTIC FANTASTIC

Plastic is very useful, but when we throw it away we create waste that hangs around for hundreds of years. Plastic can be fantastic, but only when we reuse it!

Use your pens and pencils to decorate this plastic cup.
Turn it into something beautiful that can be washed and refilled again and again.

WE NOW USE AROUND 20 TIMES MORE PLASTIC THAN WE DID 50 YEARS AGO.

A LOT OF THE SINGLE-USE PLASTIC WASTE LEFT BY HUMANS ENDS UP IN OUR OCEANS.

OI!

TREASURE THE TREES

Trees give and do so much for our world. Can you complete the rest of the labels, writing down how each part of the tree helps planet Earth?

FRUIT provides food for us to eat.

LEAVES help to give us clean air to breathe.

BRANCHES

NUTS AND SEEDS

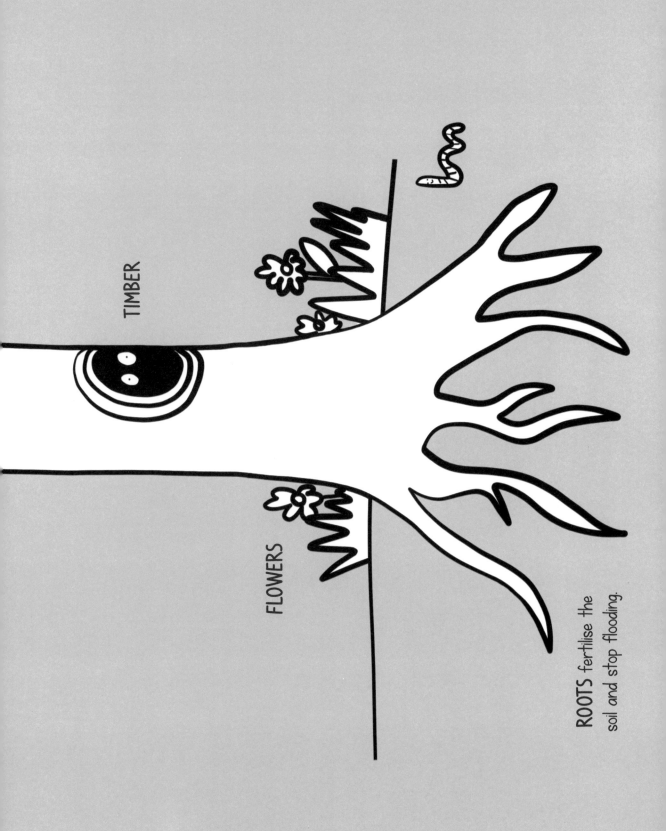

TIMBER

FLOWERS

ROOTS fertilise the soil and stop flooding.

BUY NOTHING DAY

How much do you consume and throw away in a single day? The answer probably varies on different days of the week and at different times of the year.

In wealthy parts of the world, so much waste and pollution is needless. Pick a day and ask everyone in your household to agree to make it a 'buy nothing day'.

Sit down with your family and make a list of all the things you buy in a normal week. It could include everything from your food to magazines, clothes and gifts.

For one day, make a promise to make do with what you have. Do not buy anything. How do you feel? How does the day go?

At the end of the day, make a list of the money you saved. How much time did you save from not shopping?

Now consider the future. How could you buy less and waste less in your everyday life?

WHY DO YOU THINK PEOPLE BUY SO MUCH STUFF?

DO YOU THINK THEY NEED EVERYTHING THAT THEY BUY? WHY?

THINK POSITIVE

When it comes to creating a greener, cleaner world there is a lot to do, but lots of good things are also happening every single day, right across the globe!

Fill in a sticky note every time you find out about something positive that's happening to help the environment. It could be locally or on a wider scale.

WHY NOT...
Watch the national news?
Talk to your friends?
Check out local community noticeboards?

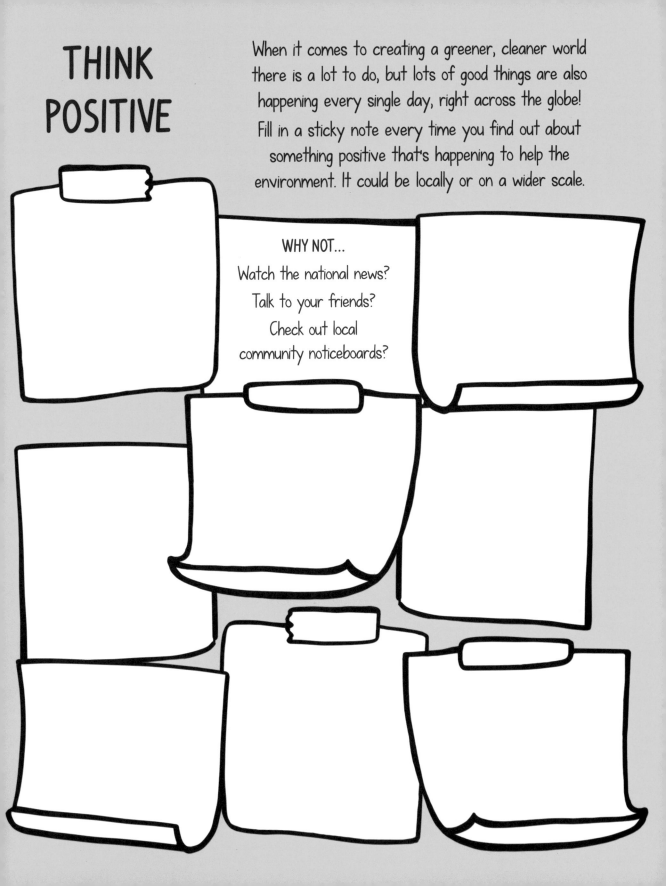

SAVE THE DATE

Earth Day is a very special annual holiday that is celebrated all around the world. It takes place every year on 22nd April. On Earth Day, global citizens come together to protect and speak up for our environment.

FEED THE BIRDS

Spread the love by sprinkling bird food in a quiet place outside.

PLANT A TREE

Get permission to plant a tree in a special place and hold a ceremony to mark the occasion.

GIVE SEED PACKETS TO YOUR FRIENDS

Make this a gift on Earth Day and provide the opportunity to grow new plants to enjoy.

GO FOR A NATURE WALK

Explore a trail or path, taking in every tiny detail.

EARTH DAY IS MARKED BY ROUGHLY ONE BILLION PEOPLE FROM 192 COUNTRIES AROUND THE WORLD.

Will you join the celebrations? Why not host an eco-friendly Earth Day party with your friends or family?

Try these ideas out or think up some new ones of your own.

Colour in your favourite ideas.

COOK AND SHARE SOME FOOD OUTSIDE

Eating outside is always magical! Sit, eat and share your thoughts about our wonderful world.

WATCH THE SUNSET TOGETHER

Or if you get up early, maybe watch the sunrise!

UNPLUG FROM ALL THINGS TECH

Put your gadgets to one side for a whole day.

ENJOY A SPECIAL VIEW

Stand on top of a hill, go to the beach or climb a tree.

EARTH DAY WANTS TO GET THE WORD OUT – IT'S TIME FOR ALL OF US TO CARE ABOUT THE ENVIRONMENT!

CHANGES

Sometimes change is hard, but the results can be amazing!

How have your thoughts and habits changed as you've grown?

Fill in the boxes, then colour in the beautiful butterflies.

How have your actions changed?

How have your ideas changed since you started writing in this book?

What would you like to change in the future?

How can you persuade others to change?

IF THERE WAS NO CHANGE, THERE WOULDN'T BE ANY BUTTERFLIES

JOY FROM JUNK

Junk modelling is an amazing way to recycle! All you need is sticky tape, scissors and some pens to decorate your creations.

1. Collect a pile of old cardboard boxes and rescue some other materials from the recycling bin. Make sure that everything you pick is clean and safe to use.

2. Decide what you would like to make. The more fantastical the better!

3. Start sticking your model together.

GREAT MODELLING MATERIALS

- Egg boxes
- Cereal boxes
- Silver foil
- Shoeboxes
- Lolly sticks
- Cotton reels
- Sweet wrappers
- Cardboard tubes
- Bubble wrap
- Buttons
- Scraps of cloth
- Drinks cartons
- Rubber gloves

Always check with an adult before you start a new craft project. Stay safe with scissors.

WHEN YOU'VE FINISHED WITH YOUR JUNK MODEL, DRAW A PICTURE OF IT HERE, THEN YOU CAN BREAK IT UP AND START AGAIN, OR KEEP IT AS A WORK OF ART!

PLOT IT OUT

Growing seeds is fun, but it can also be fruitful.
A veggie garden can provide all sorts
of tasty things to eat.
Use your drawing skills to fill this plot
with herbs, vegetables and fruit.

Ask a teacher if your class can grow a
vegetable garden at school. With lots of
hands to help, there is less work to do.

WHY NOT SEW...?

carrots	lettuces
beans	marrows
radishes	sunflowers
strawberries	herbs
peas	mint

If your school is short on space, you could grow plants in pots instead.

Take turns watering the plants, weeding the plot and harvesting your crops.

POLAR PICTURE

The Arctic is the cold and snowy area around the North Pole.

Climate change is affecting this part of the world. As temperatures increase more and more, ice is starting to melt.

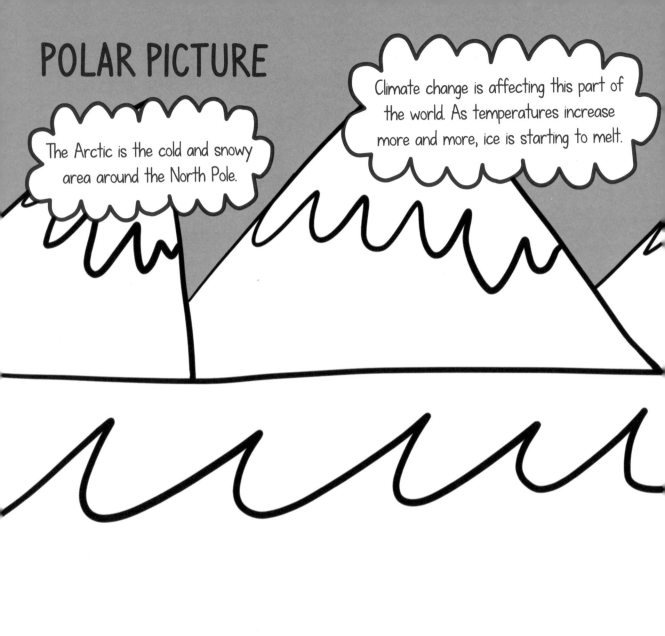

ORCA

SEAL

MOOSE

WALRUS

REINDEER

PUFFIN

POLAR BEAR

NARWHAL

PROJECT PROTECT

Many animal species living today are endangered and some have already become extinct. Human beings and their actions are the biggest threat that animals face today.

THE TYPE OF ANIMAL I WANT TO PROTECT IS:

....

DRAW A PICTURE OF IT HERE:

DRAW AN ARROW TO SHOW WHERE THIS ANIMAL LIVES:

As we spread out across more and more of the planet, we destroy natural habitats, making it very difficult for some species to survive.

Do your bit to find out about animal conservation! Pick an endangered species that you care about, then find out about it either online or at the library.

Now write about it on these project pages.

Reasons why this animal is endangered:

Three things that I can do to help:

This animal is amazing because:

FOOD CHAINS

All living things need energy to live.

They get this from food.

Plants make their own food from sunlight, but animals and humans need to eat other animals and plants to get their energy to survive.

They are all part of a food chain.

A food chain shows how plants and animals depend on each other.

There are food chains everywhere – both on the land and in the ocean.

SUN

GRASS

CRICKET

EAGLE

SNAKE

BIRD

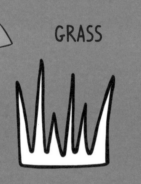

PLANKTON

LARGER FISH

SHARK

ALGAE

SMALL FISH

SEA LION

Can you draw another food chain here?

You could think about creatures of the African savannah or the Amazon rainforest...

Plants are called PRODUCERS because they make their own food.

Animals are CONSUMERS. They eat plants and other animals.

SPREAD THE WORD

Being green is not only about taking action, but also inspiring and encouraging others to do the same. Fill the empty speech bubbles with shout-outs to help to lead even more people towards becoming global citizens.

Can you draw features on all of the faces?

Together, Everyone Achieves More

Don't be the same. Be better!

Turn these characters into your classmates, sports team or even your family members.

Teamwork is everything!

RECYCLING REMINDER

Design a poster to show what can be recycled in your household. Add colour, tips and pictures to help your family to remember to do their bit and reduce landfill waste.

When you've finished, cut the poster out of the book and ask an adult to stick it on the wall above your household bin.

SCHOOL SOS

Does your school need an eco-warrior?
Why not make it you? Think up some more initiatives
for making your school a greener place.

Build a nature corner for pupils, staff and wildlife to visit and enjoy.

Start a plastic bag amnesty. How quickly can your school become carrier bag-free?

Set up an eco-council. Ask a pupil from every class to join in and spread the word.

Work with the school kitchen to improve the lunchtime recycling system.

MY SCHOOL IS CALLED: _____

MY GREEN GOALS FOR IT ARE: _____

_____

_____

_____

_____

_____

I CAN SEE A RAINBOW
MAKE A BEAUTIFUL RAINBOW OUT OF OLD MAGAZINES

1

Tear up the pages of a glossy magazine or comic book into small scraps of paper.

2 Sort the scraps into coloured piles.

PAPER IS SIMPLE AND EASY TO RECYCLE. INSTEAD OF THROWING YOUR COMICS AND MAGAZINES AWAY, CONSIDER:

Using them to cover your schoolbooks

Creating zany, multicoloured bunting

Pasting them onto card to make gift tags

Cutting out headline letters and creating cool slogan posters

3 Find some glue, then stick the mini mosaic pieces onto the rainbow arch.

SWAP IT

Instead of throwing things away, swap them with your friends! The books, toys, kit and clothes you don't need can all be traded for something else.

TEDDY BEAR'S PICNIC
Love cuddly toys?
Host a picnic at your house and invite your friends to trade teddies.

FOOTBALL SWAP SHOP
Play for a football team?
Make a date to swap boots, shirts and kit that you've outgrown.

GAME TRADER
Console crazy?
When you've mastered your latest game, see if someone would like to swap with you.

BUILD EXCHANGE
Serious about building blocks?
Set up a day to exchange bricks, swapping new builds for old.

I WOULD LIKE TO SWAP:

MY SWAP WISH LIST

SWAPPING RULES

1. Check that both sides are happy before you swap.

2. Only swap items that are in good condition.

3. Make a fair trade. Items should be roughly around the same size or value.

Before you give away or exchange any of your belongings, check with an adult that it's OK.

LEAD THE WORLD

If you were a world leader, what changes would you make?

Write a bold new set of laws to make sure the future stays green!

LAWS

Draw yourself into the picture, giving a speech at a world summit.

ADOPT AN ANIMAL

Across the world, animals need our help. If you could sponsor a wild animal and help to protect that species for the future, what creature would you choose?

Draw your animal here:

Now fill in the adoption certificate.

----

is proud to adopt a

Signed ------------------

Most wildlife charities have an 'adopt an animal' scheme. It supports their conservation work worldwide.

CLEAN AIR ZONE

Clean air matters for everyone.
Towns and cities suffer the most
from poor air quality.

They get congested with cars and trucks that create fossil fuel smog, as well as being crowded with factories and other buildings.

It's time to create a clean air zone!

Fill the empty street with people-powered bikes and trikes, hybrid vehicles, electric charging points, leafy trees and anything else you can think of to make it a better place.

REEF RESCUE

The Great Barrier Reef is precious – a complex ecosystem filled with plants, sea life and amazing coral.

Look at this tired stretch of reef, then use your pens and pencils to revive it again.

The world of the coral reef is one of the most diverse environments on the planet.
Reefs are built over thousands of years by miniscule calcium-producing organisms.

Reefs are home to around 25 per cent of all marine life. They form nurseries for around a quarter of the ocean's fish.

Draw in vibrant coral, colourful marine life and shoals of shimmering fish.

HOW CAN I HELP?

- Never collect or buy pieces of coral.
- Don't put chemicals into the water cycle. Use eco-friendly products instead.
- Conserve water as much as you can.
- Make smart seafood choices.
- Only eat sustainable fish.
- If you are lucky enough to visit the reef, look but never touch.

TEAM CLEAN

Have you ever volunteered for a community clean-up? There are lots going on all over the world. Ask your family if you can join in, or even set up a clean-up of your own.

MAKE IT EVEN BETTER

Find a place that needs some love and care. It might be a stretch of beach, some woodland or even a local park.

HOW TO DO IT

Pick up any rubbish that has been left lying around, clearing a small section of ground at a time. Sort the objects you collect into disposable waste and recyclable materials such as cans, card and plastic.

WHAT TO BRING WITH YOU:

- Rubbish sacks
- Bags for recyclable objects
- Rubber gloves
- Old clothing
- Hand sanitiser
- Sunscreen
- Picnic

PLAY IT SAFE

Never do a clean-up on your own or without permission. An adult should check that the area and the rubbish left there is safe for you to collect.

MY SUPER CLEAN-UP

Write about a successful community clean-up that you helped with.

DATE: _____ LOCATION: _____

_____

THIS IS WHO CAME WITH ME: _____

BEFORE:

AFTER:

Draw the site here.

WELL DONE, GOOD JOB!

EASY ENERGY

Renewable energy is good for the environment and it cannot get used up. Solar panels, tidal power, hydropower and geothermal energy can all help to run our homes.

Help harness more renewable energy by setting up an offshore wind farm

Draw spinning wind turbines into this section of sea.

Wind power is the world's fastest-growing energy source!

HOW MUCH DO YOU KNOW ABOUT RENEWABLES?

1. What sort of energy is hydropower? _ _ _ _ _ _ _ _ _ _ _ _ _ _ _

2. What kind of materials does biomass energy use? _ _ _ _ _ _ _ _ _ _

3. How many homes can one wind turbine power? _ _ _ _ _ _ _ _ _ _

4. How does geothermal energy work? _ _ _ _ _ _ _ _ _ _ _ _ _

5. What type of power plants are scientists hoping to build in space one day?

_ _

ANSWERS: 1. Water, 2. Natural materials, 3. Up to 300, 4. It uses the heat inside the Earth, 5. Solar power stations.

MAKE A CHOICE

We can make simple choices to conserve the world's amazing resources. We can even harness the wind, sunlight and rainwater in our own homes.

Instead of using tumble dryers to dry our laundry we can hang it outside. Fill the washing line with a row of colourful socks blowing in the breeze.

OTHER BRILLIANT CHOICES AT HOME:

- Use solar-powered gadgets such as torches, lights and calculators.
- Collect rainwater for watering plants and filling birdbaths.
- Use the wind to help a scarecrow guard your veggie patch.

CARBON FOOTPRINT

Your carbon footprint is the amount of carbon dioxide and methane gas that you use by consuming energy. It takes energy to make things, run our transport system and power our homes.

Make a list of the biggest chunks of energy that you use.

Think about how often you eat meat, fly away on holiday or ride in a car.

WHY NOT...?

- Persuade your family to have a staycation instead of flying overseas.

- Save paper. Print on both sides.

- Shut down your computer every time you have finished using it.

If we reduce the energy that we use, we can reduce our carbon footprint and make the world better for everyone!

- If you are going to visit a friend nearby, ask if you can walk instead of going by car.

- Buy locally made items that haven't been shipped or freighted in from far away.

- Don't turn on the dishwasher if it is only half-full.

Make a list of ways in which you could shrink your carbon footprint.

WONDERFUL WATER

Water is everything! We get the water that we use to drink and wash in from the rain that fills our lakes and rivers, storing it up in large dams, tanks and reservoirs. Water is one of humankind's most basic needs.

1.

2.

3.

4.

5.

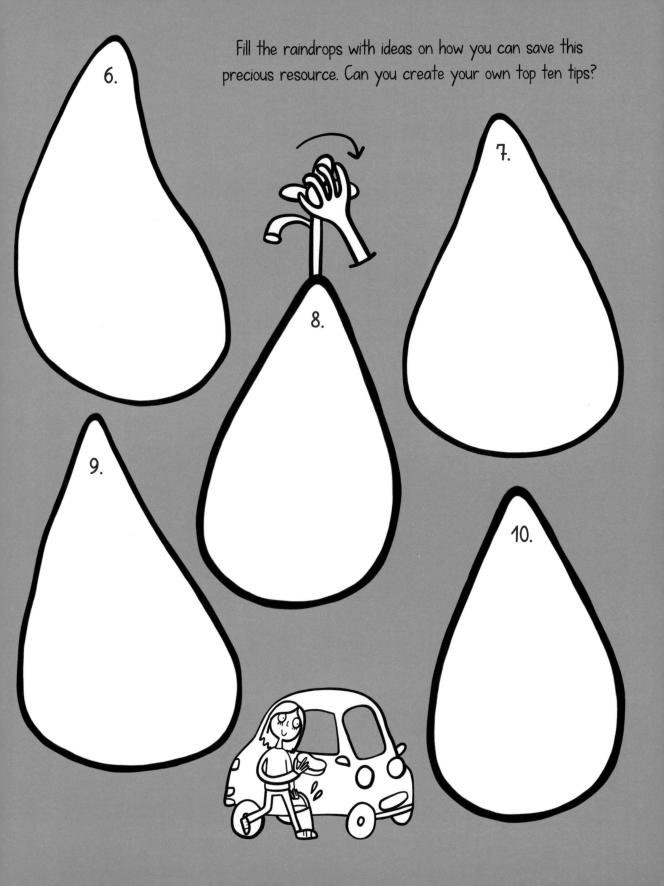

Fill the raindrops with ideas on how you can save this precious resource. Can you create your own top ten tips?

6.

7.

8.

9.

10.

T-SHIRT BOUTIQUE

Use your pens and pencils to customise the rows of old blank T-shirts into a set of eye-popping fashion statements!

CUSTOMISE YOUR TIRED TEES

Instead of throwing them out, ask permission to revamp some of your old tops. Here are some ideas to try:

- Snip the bottom hem of the T-shirt to create a fringing effect.

- Draw pictures on the T-shirt using fabric pens.

- Sew on sequins and buttons.

- Iron on a transfer of your favourite TV character.

- Dye your T-shirt a fresh new colour.

- Cut off the sleeves to make a vest top.

Be scissor safe. Ask an adult to help you.

GIFTS FROM THE EARTH

Sharing is caring. Think of all the lovely gifts that the planet gives us every single day!
Fill in each label with a gift from the natural world that is special to you.

What gift makes you smile most?
A stroll along the beach, the fragrance of a
lovely flower or perhaps a cuddle with your pet…

LISTEN UP

Being green is important and action needs to happen right now! Let's spread the word.

Create a trail of 'noise' coming out of this megaphone.

Write down a stirring speech or fill the page with short thoughts on why change must happen.

ONE SHORT HOUR

Earth Hour is a special event for global citizens organised every year by the World Wildlife Fund.

It's a dazzling way of showing our support for this amazing planet!

For one hour in March, millions of people all around the world switch off their lights and take some time to think about the Earth's future. Why don't you join in, too?

Switching off lights is a simple way that we can all help. Only 10 per cent of the electricity that a bulb uses actually creates light – the rest is lost as heat. Make a light switch plate to remind your family to turn off the lights every time they leave the room.

MAKE IT PERSONAL

Cut out the light switch plates, or trace the shape onto a blank piece of paper. If the template doesn't fit, you could measure your light switch and create your own!

Decorate the plates with coloured pens, adding a clear message to switch off.

Use double-sided sticky tape to fix your design to the light switch.

Check with an adult before you start cutting and sticking.

SINGLE LIGHT SWITCH

DOUBLE LIGHT SWITCH

BIG WIDE WORLD

The world is a vast place with many kinds of breathtaking wonders. Which environments would you like to explore?

Desert, mountain, snow or shore – tick the places you'd most like to visit, then add more of your own.

☐ THE NORTHERN LIGHTS, ICELAND

☐ GRAND CANYON, USA

☐ VICTORIA FALLS, ZIMBABWE AND ZAMBIA

☐ ULURU, AUSTRALIA

☐ TABLE MOUNTAIN, SOUTH AFRICA

☐ THE CHOCOLATE HILLS, THE PHILIPPINES

☐ SAHARA DESERT, AFRICA

☐ THE GIANT'S CAUSEWAY, NORTHERN IRELAND

If you don't know some of these places, look them up at the library or go online.

Now draw and colour some postcards from the places you'd most like to visit!

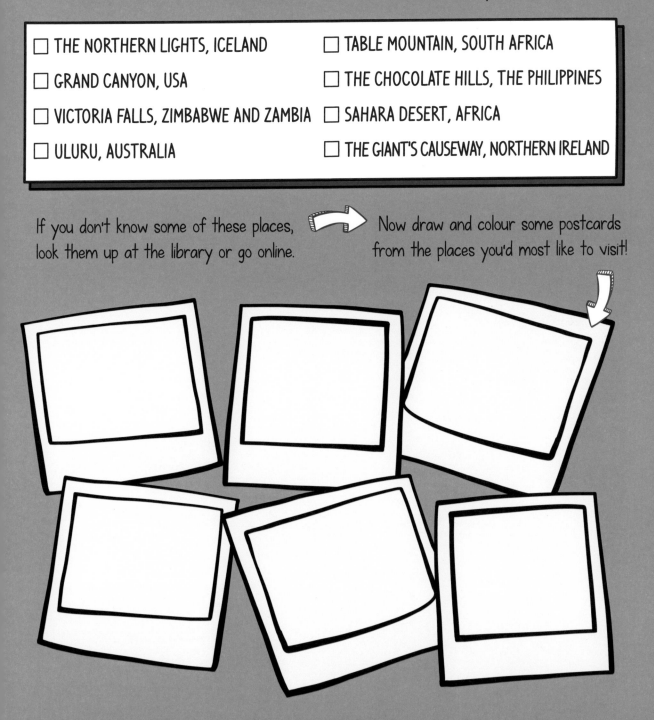

RICH RAINFOREST

The Amazon is the world's largest tropical rainforest and yet it is under threat.

Colour in this lush rainforest scene, adding as many tropical animals as you can.

The Amazon is known as the 'lungs of the Earth'. Its thick forest trees produce 20 per cent of the planet's oxygen.

A quarter of the ingredients in medicines come from rainforest plants.

Here are some creatures you might want to add:

TOUCAN

TREE FROG

JAGUAR

BLUE MORPHO BUTTERFLY

SLOTH

ANACONDA

SPIDER MONKEY

ANTEATER

IGUANA

GOLIATH BEETLE

... but there are lots, lots more!

When it rains, the tree canopy is so thick that it takes 10 minutes to reach the forest floor.

BEE HAPPY

It's time to say thank you to bees!

As well as making delicious honey, bees help to pollinate much of the food that we eat and the crops that farmers sew.

Colour in each petal, then draw a stripy honey bee, buzzing in to pollinate the flower.

Honey bees produce two to three times more honey than they need.

Around 50,000 insects live in a bee colony.

LET'S PROTECT OUR BRILLIANT BEES

They can fly at 25 km/h!

A honey bee visits between 50 and 100 flowers on each flight.

Honey does not spoil. It can last for years and years.

Bees are the only insect that produces food eaten by humans.

HONEYCOMB HOME

This colony of bees is making a honeycomb.

The hexagonal shapes can hold the queen bee's eggs, and store the pollen and honey that the workers bring to the hive.

Give the bees a hand by filling the rest of the page with honeycomb.

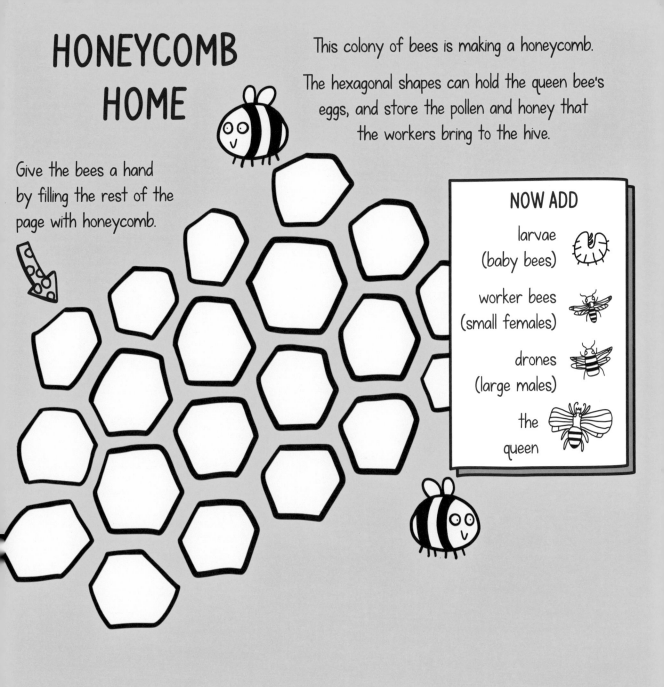

NOW ADD

larvae
(baby bees)

worker bees
(small females)

drones
(large males)

the
queen

All over the world, bee populations are in danger from loss of habitat, pesticides used on crops and climate change. There is a lot we can do to help them.

Look up organisations such as Friends of the Earth's Bee Cause!

PLANT A BEE GARDEN

Do your bit for bees by creating a mini habitat for both them and other pollinators to visit.

Ask an adult if you can create a habitat to encourage bees to visit. You could plant bee-friendly flowers in a garden, a window box or a planter.

Choose a sheltered, sunny place.

Plant the space with flowering plants and herbs. Bees like single-headed flowers like daisies and marigolds.

Look after your plants, watering them regularly. Water helps plants to produce nectar.

Don't use poisonous weedkillers or pesticides.

Try to plant a few different types of flowers, so that your space will be in bloom for as much of the year as possible.

Make a little bee bath for your garden. Fill a small pot with twigs and pebbles for the bees to perch on, then add water.

Sit back and watch. The colour and scent will soon attract a host of pollinating insects.

PICTURE THIS

Write a rebus letter using pictures, telling everyone your green dream for the future.

A rebus uses pictures in place of words.

For example, if you went for a walk on a sunny day, you could draw a stick man walking instead of the word 'walk' and a yellow sun instead of the word 'sunny'.

How many pictures can you work into your letter?

ECO-WARRIOR

When you're green, you are already a superhero!

Design a costume worthy of an eco-warrior, then think of an emblem to represent your cause.

MY ECO-WARRIOR NAME IS:

_ _ _ _ _ _ _ _ _ _ _ _ _ _ _ _

MY ECO-POWERS ARE:

_ _ _ _ _ _ _ _ _ _ _
_ _ _ _ _ _ _ _ _ _ _
_ _ _ _ _ _ _ _ _ _ _
_ _ _ _ _ _ _ _ _ _ _
_ _ _ _ _ _ _ _ _ _ _

I'M ON THE SIDE OF RIGHT BECAUSE:

_ _ _ _ _ _ _ _ _
_ _ _ _ _ _ _ _ _
_ _ _ _ _ _ _ _ _
_ _ _ _ _ _ _ _ _
_ _ _ _ _ _ _ _ _
_ _ _ _ _ _ _ _ _

THE ENEMIES I FACE EVERY DAY ARE: _ _ _ _ _ _ _

_ _ _ _ _ _ _ _ _ _ _ _ _ _ _ _ _ _ _ _
_ _ _ _ _ _ _ _ _ _ _ _ _ _ _ _ _ _ _ _

Write and draw a comic strip about your eco-warrior adventures.

Who will you take on in your battle to save the planet?

THE
END

A SECOND CHANCE

We all love pets, but rather than buy an animal, it is kinder to rehome an animal if you can.

What stray animal would you like to welcome into your family?

Draw a picture of it here!

Thousands of cats, dogs, small pets and even horses get abandoned or given away each year.

Charities like the Blue Cross try to find the happy homes that all unwanted animals deserve.

MARCHING MESSAGES

We can achieve so much more when we work as a team! Join this campaign for a greener world by writing mottos on the banners and placards.

PATCHWORK QUILT

Clothes can be saved and reused in so many ways.

This patchwork quilt has been made from old clothes that no one wants to wear any more.

Use your creative skills to decorate, colour and embellish the quilt so that every square becomes a miniature work of art.

FOUR SEASONS...

... ON ONE PAGE!

Our environment alters with the passing of the seasons.

How do the seasons change in your part of the world?

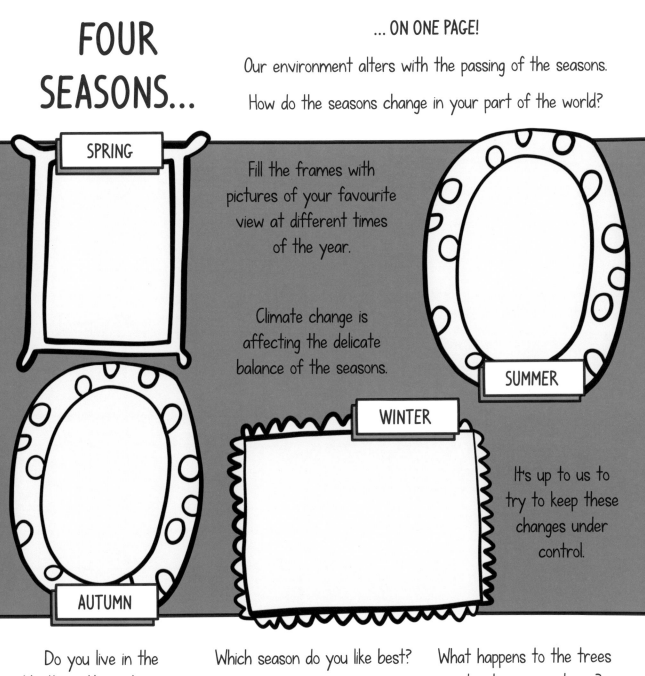

SPRING

Fill the frames with pictures of your favourite view at different times of the year.

Climate change is affecting the delicate balance of the seasons.

SUMMER

WINTER

It's up to us to try to keep these changes under control.

AUTUMN

Do you live in the Northern Hemisphere or the Southern Hemisphere?

_ _ _ _ _ _ _ _ _ _ _ _ _

_ _ _ _ _ _ _ _ _ _ _ _ _

Which season do you like best?

_ _ _ _ _ _ _ _ _ _ _ _ _

What is the temperature like then?

_ _ _ _ _ _ _ _ _ _ _ _ _

What happens to the trees and nature around you?

_ _ _ _ _ _ _ _ _ _ _ _ _

_ _ _ _ _ _ _ _ _ _ _ _ _

WEATHER WATCH

Track a month near your home, carefully recording the temperature and rainfall.

Are the results constant or unpredictable?

MAKE YOUR OWN THERMOMETER BOX

1. Find a sturdy white box.

2. Fix your thermometer inside the back of the box with reusable putty.

3. Choose a shady place outside to keep your box. Stand it up so the thermometer is upright and protected from extremes of wind, snow and rain.

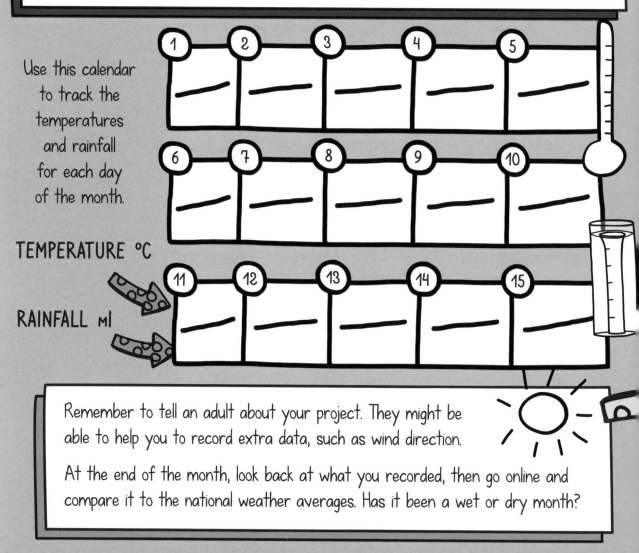

Use this calendar to track the temperatures and rainfall for each day of the month.

1 2 3 4 5

6 7 8 9 10

TEMPERATURE °C

11 12 13 14 15

RAINFALL ml

Remember to tell an adult about your project. They might be able to help you to record extra data, such as wind direction.

At the end of the month, look back at what you recorded, then go online and compare it to the national weather averages. Has it been a wet or dry month?

MAKE YOUR OWN RAIN GAUGE

1. Cut the top third off a plastic bottle. Turn the top part of the bottle upside down and push it inside the bottom section.

2. Dig a small hole and set the rain gauge into the ground. This will stop it from blowing away on windy days.

3. Check the gauge every day. Tip out the rainwater into a measuring jug and record your results.

If you don't have your own space to dig in, set your rain gauge inside a plant pot instead, or ask if you can do the experiment at school.

16 17 18 19 20 21

22 23 24 25 26

27 28 29 30 31

Weather watching becomes even more interesting when you have data to look back on and compare. Why not add extra pages on plain paper and extend your research for another month or even a full year?

SPOTTING PATTERNS

How might your results connect to reported trends in climate change?

COLOUR THIS IN:

START
WHERE YOU
ARE; USE WHAT
YOU HAVE; DO
WHAT YOU CAN!

THE SKY'S THE LIMIT

Sometimes it can be hard to see what one person can do to make the world better, but every global citizen matters!

We all look up at the same stars and we all share the same blue sky.

When you're feeling low, fill the clouds with motivational quotes to get you smiling again.

FEELING INSPIRED?

Write to your local councillor or politician about the green issue that matters most to you. Who knows what your pen power can do?

DOUBLE DENIM

When your jeans have been ripped one too many times, don't throw them away.

Ask an adult to help you to turn them into vintage denim items that all your friends will love.

Love designer gear?

You need to start upcycling!
Here are some ideas for you to think about.

DENIM BAG

Cut off the legs then use your sewing skills to create a handy shopping bag.

CUT-OFF SHORTS

They can be as long or as short as you like!

BRACELETS

Customise strips of denim with buttons, ribbon and sequins.

NOTEBOOK COVER

Keep the pockets in place to make handy storage compartments.

BEDROOM BINS

Wrap the jeans fabric around a bin.

COLLAGE ART

Get creative with glue, scissors and scraps of material.

PARTY BUNTING

Cut out triangles of denim then decorate them with colourful letters and attach them to a length of ribbon.

ROOM TIDY

Mount it on your wall, then fill it with stationery.

Denim is a heavy fabric that can be difficult to cut.

Be careful when using sharp scissors.

THAT'S A FACT

Some amazing statistics are emerging about the Earth and how it is changing.

Scientists are discovering new things every day.

Each time you hear a jaw-dropping fact or figure, write it here so you remember.

ONE WORLD

We can discover so much more about our world by learning from other cultures.

How are people on the other side of the planet coping with climate change and its consequences?

Choose a faraway part of the world that interests you.

Go online, visit the library and talk to your teacher to find out more.

Bring back your knowledge and share it here:

SOME PEOPLE AND PLACES TO FIND OUT ABOUT:

Aboriginal people of Australia

Nomads in Mongolia

City workers in Tokyo, Japan

Tribespeople in the Amazon rainforest

TIME CAPSULE

What's your message to the next generation of global citizens?

Write it into the time capsule below.

You could draw pictures and photos to record what life is like on Earth now.

_____ 'S TIME CAPSULE

DO NOT READ UNTIL: _____

MY GREEN MESSAGE FOR THE FUTURE IS:

_____

_____

_____

_____

DATE: _____

When you have finished, cut the page out and lock it somewhere safe and dry.
Maybe someone will open it up and read it in a few years' time!

MY PLEDGE TO BE GREEN

Tick the boxes and add your own pledges to create your own green promise,
then decorate the document with beautiful animals and flowers.

I, _____,

promise to be a green global citizen.

I will try to:

☐ Be kind to animals

☐ Reduce my carbon footprint

☐ Buy products with less packaging

☐ Eat local organic food

☐ Look after nature

☐ Reduce, reuse, recycle

Signed _____

THE BIT FOR GROWN UPS

This activity book is perfect for parents, teachers, learning mentors, caregivers, therapists, social workers and youth leaders who want to help children to understand the importance of our environment and their place as global citizens.

As we move through the 21st century, preserving our environment and its fragile ecosystems is becoming a more and more pressing concern. It is an issue that affects everyone, and one that is being led from the front by children and young people all over the world.

Children are learning about green issues at school, talking about it with their friends, and hearing about themes such as climate change and pollution through social media and the news. Many can recognise that green policies, or a lack of them, will have an impact on their future. As parents, adult relatives and friends, we need to find ways to support our young people, talk with them about their concerns and look at how we can work together to make the world a greener, more sustainable place.

This book offers children the chance to find out more about different environmental issues and explore what it really means to 'be green'. The fun activities will show them the value of small but positive action and demonstrate the interconnectivity of life, as well as allowing them to express their worries and concerns.

As a responsible adult, there are all sorts of things that you can do to support children as they find out about being green. Give children the space they need to talk about any fears for the future, and try to model good eco-citizenship and respect for the planet. It's fine if environmental considerations are new to you, too, as you can share conversations and find out information together.

FREECYCLE

The Freecycle Network is made up of millions of members around the world. It's a grassroots and entirely non-profit movement of people who are giving (and receiving) items for free in their own areas, keeping useful objects out of landfills.

www.freecycle.org

FRIENDS OF THE EARTH

An international community dedicated to protecting the natural world and the well-being of all of its inhabitants. Friends of the Earth leads campaigns, provides resources and information, and drives real solutions to the environmental problems facing us all.

www.friendsoftheearth.uk

GREENPEACE

Defends the natural world and promotes peace by investigating, exposing and confronting environmental abuse, while championing responsible solutions for our fragile environment.

www.greenpeace.org.uk

THE YOUNG PEOPLE'S TRUST FOR THE ENVIRONMENT

The YPTE is a charity that aims to encourage young people's understanding of the environment and the need for sustainability.

www.ypte.org.uk